WALKING UPHILL AT NOON

MARY BURRITT CHRISTIANSEN POETRY SERIES
Hilda Raz, Series Editor

The Mary Burritt Christiansen Poetry Series publishes two to four books a year that engage and give voice to the realities of living, working, and experiencing the West and the Border as places and as metaphors. The purpose of the series is to expand access to, and the audience for, quality poetry, both single volumes and anthologies, that can be used for general reading as well as in classrooms.

ALSO AVAILABLE IN THE
MARY BURRITT CHRISTIANSEN POETRY SERIES:

The Loneliest Girl: Poems by Kate Gale
origin story: poems by Gary Jackson
Nowhere: Poems by Katie Schmid
The Definition of Empty: Poems by Bill O'Neill
Ancestral Demon of a Grieving Bride: Poems by Sy Hoahwah
Feel Puma: Poems by Ray Gonzalez
Grief Land: Poems by Carrie Shipers
The Shadowgraph: Poems by James Cihlar
Crosscut: Poems by Sean Prentiss
The Music of Her Rivers: Poems by Renny Golden

For additional titles in the Mary Burritt Christiansen Poetry Series, please visit unmpress.com.

WALKING UPHILL AT NOON

POEMS

jon kelly yenser

university of new mexico press / albuquerque

Printed in the United States of America

Library of Congress Cataloging-in-Publication data
is on file with the Library of Congress

ISBN 978-0-8263-6373-2 (paper)
ISBN 978-0-8263-6374-9 (e-book)

Founded in 1889, the University of New Mexico sits on the traditional homelands of the Pueblo of Sandia. The original peoples of New Mexico—Pueblo, Navajo, and Apache—since time immemorial have deep connections to the land and have made significant contributions to the broader community statewide. We honor the land itself and those who remain stewards of this land throughout the generations and also acknowledge our committed relationship to Indigenous peoples. We gratefully recognize our history.

Cover illustration: "Completed Moment," 18" x 18",
mixed media on wood by Terry Gloeckler
Designed by Mindy Basinger Hill
Composed in Arno Pro Regular and Bebas Neue

FOR PAMELA *as always* FOR STEPHEN *my brother* FOR JUDY *in memory*

CONTENTS

three HEALTHY LIVING

four THE ARTS

LOCAL NEWS ONE

GARBAGE

Here's hoping no one
shoots the coyote that sorts
our trash on Tuesdays

cantering sideways
can to can, picking, choosing,
since he has the time

it's so early no
one sees him limping, bony
like all coyotes

but I worry some
drunk or some insomniac
will take note, decide

to save our neighbors
from the only animal
we've all satisfied.

ROSES BLOOM IN THE ALLEY

A boy and girl came down the alley
carrying what they owned in a backpack
and plastic bags. From the kitchen galley
I heard him: "Wow."
                    The girl in her tracks

stooped and then a long "ooh." It was the roses,
I knew, and stepped outside.
                              "We were just ad . . ."
he began. "I know," I said, "those yellows
on the back wall, the ones climbing like mad,

are called Lady Banks and these,"
pointing to the bush where the girl stood,
"Fourth of July."
                  "I get that totally,"
she said, "like little fireworks. That's good."

"Take one, but mind the thorns."
                                  She took
a step forward, bent in, then quickly back,
blood on her lip. "I bit it off." She shook
the stem and bloom and fixed it all in her black

black hair—a small explosion in a night sky.
"Thanks."
          "No . . . it's you," I said. "Good-bye."

OWL MADE IN CHINA

Not just his head—his whole body—swivels
a full 360 like a toy—not your standard owl.
But the point is not so much verisimilitude
as vigilance, a good spin whenever the wind
picks up, catching the rudder glued
on his back like a freakish wing. His eyes
that once were yellow as yolks have dimmed—
he has no down time, no nest in the piñon,
sitting all hours on *latillas* where pigeons
used to roost and coo and foul the patio.
By now even the savvy crows have relocated
in the elm, leaving just the oblivious
hummingbirds in the penstemon below,
fizzing bloom to bloom like bloody yo-yos.

END OF THE WEEKEND

She imagines the neighbors watching
across Amherst Street and wishes
the day over. There's still unpacking
to do—the bronze SUV shimmering
with dust, three doors open and the hatch
sprung out—a great bug too heavy
to lift off.
What must they think?
She'd like
to wave and shout about how much fun
she thinks they had when the sun was out
most of the time and the creek riffling.

Right now she needs help. And here he comes.
She does not dress her husband, of course,
but she could do better than this—his shorts
have too many pockets and zippers
and the khaki's worn too soft for creasing.
At least he's put his shirt on.

But where are the children? There must be
children—otherwise no point having
a vehicle this size that does not fit
the driveways of our bungalows,
which are modest and, but for the occasional porch
painted turquoise, largely colorless.

This family is exhausted but not done:
a broken trike and plastic tubs
of toy cars and trucks. A Coleman stove.
The children must be bundled in back,
strapped in their seats. They'll be last,
a little burned and itching with chiggers,
too sleepy for Grimm when the time comes.

Dusk. She hears the neighbors' terrier
yapping, yapping at the front window,
but they have stopped watching now.
It's time for supper and news from the world,
and they're no longer curious about her kids,
about his dreadful clothes.

OSPREY ON THE STREAM

Headlong for miles upstream and full
of stones, at last the water flattens
and backs up on the other bank,
undercut, a pool deeper, greener
than any so far, the day's last spot,
an hour to work the run.
An osprey
sitting cockeyed at the top of a snag
watches me wade midway and thread
a mayfly onto a tippet so thin
I fumble it twice while cutthroat begin
breaking the surface now and now again
until the pool is dimpled everywhere.
The hatch rises, a dusty scrim.
I play out line and loop it and make
a false cast before the osprey has seen
enough: impatient, indelicate, oblivious
to drift, he lifts off, hovers and flops
headfirst and then flaps up, the last fish
caught today in his balled claws.

THE PILL

Saving the best for last   for the dulling
for the getting down from the edgy ups
of pain   ridges of needles   abrupt scarp
whetted rocks like coral   a bone-dry gulley.

I start home   back to the expanse
of wheat fields in full sun
where a breeze combing the rows in turn
proves something's alive in Kansas.

And farther back   the half-dark cellar
of the house on Coolidge: listen to the swishing
the thrumming   the waltz of the washing machine
my mother's Bendix rocking   ajar

watching me with a blurred   hypnotic eye.
I thank memories of pain as pain goes by.

ROAD TRIP HOME

—for Betty Moffett

We cruise through Kismet without a thought
of easing off or shifting down: no limit,
no stoplight, one corner, two silos
the other end of town. You know what they say,
"if you blink" or "just a wide spot."

Behind us: Oklahoma's red dirt
and flocks of pumpjacks pecking
in the scrub, a few kinks in the two-lane,
a slight rise, a slight fall. But now, order
put to the fields—planted, squared off.

We cross once the dry wash
of the Cimarron and seven times
the muddy Ninnescah. Passing one road
to Auntie Em's and another promising
the Daltons' desperado hideout

not much arrests the eye
except the hawk that banks an updraft
and sees all of it at once, like god: the shrill
killdeer nesting in the weeds and each crow
back and forth from spattered roadkill

to blasted cottonwood and every rodent
quickening in the spring wheat.

WHAT SHE SAID

Apropos.
Be of good cheer.
Comparisons are odious.
DT's can kill you, I assure you.
Every time I quit was the last time.
Floors me! Simply floors me.
Gee, babe, ain't I good to you?
He was probably eyeing you, too.
I will kill myself.
Joining AA kept my friends close.
Kelly—because you came out scrunched, a little red Irishman.
Living with your father was my chance to know someone else.
My first year nursing, I couldn't see anyone's face.
"No one" takes a singular. It means not any *one*. Ditto "everyone."
Ola, your grandma, shot a man in western Kansas.
Phenobarb for short.
Quentin must be my favorite Faulkner character.
Remember: Miss Wichita of 1938 was my dear friend.
Sherman's name was never said aloud in Atlanta.
Tickled. Simply tickled. Sometimes pink.
Uncle JD, scoundrel that he was, was a handsome man.
Very.
Why should I? I was no happier sober.
X who lived in Oklahoma adored me half my life.
You mean I never told you? I meant to. Gad-
zooks! she said back then. God's wounds.

SUNDAYS IN WICHITA

After Willard's solo at Woodland Church—
            Were You There? or Steal Away,
            or too often The Battle Hymn,
with the flock coming in

every chorus—after the short walk home,
            the long decline of afternoon
            dispute begins. But first a round
of highballs in the front room, tumblers

sweating circles on TV trays, pressed board
            printed with mallards
            northward, a sky clear
except for the laminate tears.

Framed on the mantle with his wings,
            Uncle Steve, his airman's cap
            raked left, a crisp bombardier
long lost over water, keeps watch.

Drinks freshened. Rattles in the kitchen:
            potatoes boiling, the chicken
            floured and shaken in a sack.
In deep heat the cicadas' dizzy rounds.

Now Willard chuckles, "Show-me, I guess
            old Harry S. showed 'em, all right!"
            And Betty answers, "It's a shame.
"All those children," Betty says, "Generations."

"Had to be done," he says. "American boys . . ."
            "Don't tell me!" she says. "How dare you?
            You with your essential job. My own brother . . ."
She looks at the mantle. "My blood."

So on like that. Sometimes more,
          sometimes less. A last shot
          before supper: "Patton
was a great man." "No, he was not."

We move to the mahogany table: Pabst
          on ice (all this before AC),
          Jell-O molded, potatoes mashed,
drumsticks bloody on the bone.

HERE WE ARE IN HELL

This is our gravelly ground of play—
Woodland School, 1957,
its outdoor equipment ironclad:
climbing bars, jungle gym, the giant
with its awful, greasy chains ratcheting
overhead, busting shins and elbows
and now and then a skull. The boys
favor it, and the girls who don't mind
their dirty bottoms up. Getting on
is the trick—timing and luck: you run
in circles in the dusty rut, dodging rungs
until you jump to grab one. Sometimes
it works. Otherwise, you duck, scramble,
hunker down for another round.

Under that pair of oaks we ambushed
and depantsed Louis Royston for no reason
and ran his jeans up the flagpole. For one thing,
he was a new kid, timid, thin-limbed.
For another, he lived in a duplex
without a father. A decade later he left—
upright marine and soon enough came back
in a coffin. For no reason. You know kids.
Sharon had the cooties and Kendra was
the teacher's pet. On that corner Billy Phillips
showed us rubbers he saved in a cigar box.
Now, for the sake of safety, the equipment's gone.
We could have stayed longer: James and Louis
and Frankie who lost his head in the highlands.

NATURAL LAW IN THE NEIGHBORHOOD

It was Larry Allen underneath the street lamp
at 14th and Julianne, where the bats gathered
at nightfall for the moths, who said, "Have you
ever seen your parents doing it, you know,

or thought about Gramma going at it with Gramps?"
Considering, I watched the feeding bats.
"Have you ever seen Sue Blonsky naked?"
he asked. "Because I have. Plenty."
That's a lie

right there, I said, who liked that girl who happened
to live just down the street from where we stood.
Larry said, "Let's take the alley and you'll see."
So we went, lifting lightly our feet off the gravel

and we crawled through the hole in the fence
Larry had cut some time before.
Her curtains were drawn. Still we lay a long time
in the grass while the chiggers chewed their way in.

THE GOSSIP IN WICHITA IN 1963

for MVW

One cloudy day in Wichita
one day in autumn
a clabbered sky.

Imagine an involved compass
of geese wheeling south   delible prints
offering distance and a hint

of loss for those of us whose narratives
kept wavering.
What happened or might have

that night at Judy's: our brutish painter
was needling you. "You have tiny
hands. Like a girl!"
What if

he had tilted you from your chair   tequila
spilling down your pants
embarrassing all of us?

I can't imagine   let alone recall exactly
what did happen   but there were no stains.
He set your chair down.

The next summer you left
for Mexico with him and his girlfriend
and every year thereafter

for a decade. And what if that canvas
of his (a girl like a bird, a bird
like a thorn, a touch of Redon)

had not been stolen by long-legged Sharon
          (whose wholly un-muscled body
                    in all its chill was the model)?

Sharon hung it in her awful walk-up.
                              What if
          someone we didn't know had snatched it
                    insulting us all?

We would have been thieves. Sharon ran off
          with our novelist. I watched it all.
                    But what if the president

had not been shot that fall
          on a cloudy day that was brilliant
                    at once? I know

where I was: drinking with Sharon
          and trying to get lucky
                    with the usual result.

That's how I remember it:
          layered as the plot might seem.
                    Something else: I remember

a day of clouds   the air withdrawn
          to the tops of nearly leafless elms.
                    I was looking for a story

up there   a second breath
          something none of us had thought of.
                    I have told this story too often.

THESE DAYS

—In Memory of Harvey White

I think Harvey must be settled
by now, no longer uneasy
in his digs.
                    I think about those days
when he told me from time to time
he would have to beat me down
in the streets, *if it comes to it.*
To a pulp, he said, that is,
if it comes to it. A man of good size,
he could have done so.
                                        He said that
some mornings when we sat
in the union drinking coffee
and smoking Marlboros.
                                            He said
maybe we should all vote
for Governor Wallace, for the sake
of clarity.
                You could never do that,
I said.
            Are you kidding?

Most lunch hours we played hoops
in the old gym.
                            For dinner
we ate ham sandwiches
and baskets of chips at a bar
called The Hut, where his friend
Lester played a random bass
in a funk band.

Man, Harve said,
if he misses one more change
I'll have to thump him.
He was kidding, of course.
He would never thump Lester
for the obvious, good reason.
I understand all this better now.
I trust Harvey is easy.

CONCERNING CERTAIN DEATHS IN RURAL AMERICA

At first you think it's amusing.
But the list keeps growing until
chills come on because
death happens out here,
every so often freakishly. Item:
falling into a half-full, slowly filling
grain elevator the seasonal boy suffocates
hours before he's dug out
in the middle of the night in Iowa. Item:
just stepping down from a circling tractor
kills another kid who catches his pants
last thing. It happens in the fall in Kansas.
More than once a year something explodes in the barn.
No one hears it in the rain,
or you think it's thunder. Or lightning strikes the boy
playing left field in the pasture—
quirky tale actually true this time:
Roscoe, it was, cousin on mother's side.
Some deaths *are* normal, but there's no doubt
the local section prefers those accidents
uniquely rural or the occasional
very suspicious one. For instance:
when Walter's wife said he seized up
X-mas Eve feeding the pigs and so was eaten
you simply couldn't believe her, because of all those
zeroes on his policy for a whole life.

POVERTY POINT

After we saw the bat's wing hung
on a thistle in the thick burdock,
tanned in the sun and wrinkling
like a piece of chamois cloth,
Uncle Cal found one alive

and, nudging it with his boot,
said he couldn't stand to watch
an animal, rabid or not, starve.
When the kids went off to the ruin
of the barn, he used the pistol with buckshot

and when they came running, "Oh,
let's see. . . . Oh, what happened?"
"Nothing," he said, "left to see,"
which was right except the weeds
were bent back as if windbeaten.

So one of the kids pointed down the valley
where the river winds into Iowa,
past that spit where the factory is,
at a thunderhead the color of a bruise
settling down just south of Lynxville.

EAVESDROPPING AT THE DINER

I. IMPLEMENT SALESMAN

A guy should see it coming,
the usual, you can't get over
the morning news.

You have an arresting face.
Do you have a husband at home on the farm
who can't make a living?

Do you have a headache?
I'll take the Denver omelet
and a side of *salsa verde.*

Thank you.
Do you find yourself
too often accommodating others
to a fault as I do?

I have a headache. You have
the news. You have a face
I can't get over.

What's up   what's going down   who you talkin
to fool   you   you   frontin me   do we have
direction yet   I hear you   hip   hype   hup
conjugate that   mofo   and while you're
at it   suck on this   if you're not a part
of the solution   you are the problem
word that   on the bus   off   hey oinker up
against the wall what   whatever   say what
what direction   who you talkin to   you
fool you   you down   I'm down   dawg   dog soldier
dog face   doggy style at Abu Ghraib
is how that is   how's that   howitzer's how
it is   hey-hey   free Huey   hey bring in
the Hueys   fly jiggy fly   direction that

III. NEIGHBORS

Not my skill set exactly
actually.

Ouch. Help me out
            here.

Inexactly either
in all honesty.
But still I heard
that I heard that
I heard that

long and loud.

It's just she sounds
hysterical
about half the time

I should say. I should say
          all's more like it

all's more like it
then and then there's this guy.

I know.

Several guys actually.

I know
          that I know that.

All the time's more like it.

Come on
          now come on
          be nice.

Don't have to be
do I? Are you? Of a certain age
aren't we
are we not?

We are
          actually. Honestly.

Time to turn up the heat
I'd say.

I'd say so. I'd say
so but excited.

Better said.

I'm saying use what you got
in the toolbox and whatever

and not just
that either although
you can't rule that out
can you?

Oh, no. No question.

A CALENDAR

Spring
Her lover's small pain
throbbed in her palm, fragile
as a nesting wren.

Summer
When the hatch thickens
like dust above the riffles,
mend your drifting line.

Fall
A buck the color
of slash and still where he stands
startles the hunter.

Winter
First snowfall like smoke
drifts down the hill while aspen
ignite the valley.

TRAVEL SECTION TWO

ISLAND POSTCARD

Later I bought you
a painted tile on Tinos—
thinking of you as

I do and it was
lit from within as light is
on these islands as

you know—made by hand,
nonetheless by someone else
in chalk and azure.

LATE NEWS ON PAROS

War stories end
on cracker barrels over jars
of pickled eggs or olives

vats of feta   in cafés
or bars along the volta   in this
taverna where we sit

this Saturday   watching
the market begin   bayonets
laid on blankets

in the bright sun
and Nazi helmets arrayed
on shaky tables

saved most days for old men
at dominoes and ouzo
afternoons   some of them

the very ones who collected
these leftovers from the old days
of this island

without light all hours.
We drink our Nescafé and eat
the thick yogurt

ignoring yesterday's *Herald*
set at our place   ferried over
this morning in the dark.

SPARTA AND BEYOND

In colonel country one comes
to understand "laconic."
Every few miles a billboard
celebrates in silhouette the soldiers
rising from flames in '67.

On the outskirts of this village
young boys sprint in relays
beside our borrowed Renault—
"Cinq drachs! Cinq drachs!"
Clusters of grapes swing like lanterns.

Sparta is strictly one star,
everything in bits and pieces because,
the guidebook says, an early scholar
"scattered inscriptions to increase
by rarity his finds."

But further: Mystras!
Byzantine ruins nothing
could replace—those domes,
those luminous glooms! We finish
five churches and climb

to the fortress at noon.
From here Mystras seems a bombed city.
From here the only relief from Sparta
is the occasional olive tree
exploding on the plain.

ROTOGRAVURE FROM SOUNION

It was S. who objected then,
who spoke, smiling, of a "loss
in the moment," but today the photos
we took shine back from the page
with more and less light

given the angle: "the Tholos,
a rainbow, goats on the Peloponnesus . . ."
We kept a faithful record, even the lost
exposures: "number five," P. wrote,
"is a black eye. Uncover the lens!"

Here is a series of the four
of us against a wall, a dead end
of broken columns and slabs of frieze
overarched by bougainvillea.
Forgive me for thinking I invented it all.

But if we were lost in some devious
back way—and that island *was* a maze
for pirates once, a lure
to draw them from the waterfront—
that, too, is possible: it's obvious

we lost ourselves. And those shops,
I swear, changed from day to day only
because we bought things: sandals
soled with tire rubber, straw hats,
komboloi. . . . Occasionally scenes

as they were snap back: the dazzling
pages of Greek we studied, the dizzy
switchbacks above Tripoli, the rain
at Megalopolis, a cracked bowl,
and Corinth, a field of boulders.

Still, I have my favorites:
wounded head and heel (an overhang,
a sea urchin) here I'm climbing
to Athena's temple at noon, the one
once thought to be Poseidon's.

In the next one I'm tracing "Byron,"
carved on the pillar, which is black
with 100 years of hands and lips.
In the background you can see
the site's photographer bent, focusing

on a young woman in blue chiffon,
posed against the sea and smiling
far-off. It was S. who took that picture
of us all looking different ways.
There are changes we've wanted to endure.

YOU CAN SEE ON THIS POSTCARD

—for J.

where we sat—right *there*—
playing gin on this square
in Girona where we'd come
after that confusion with tickets.

No one in this picture,
faded like silk, appears
out of place on this square
where we played gin.

We walked, too: "Tourist!
You are the terrorist!"
was sprayed on a wall on the way
to a notable church.

Of course it's not true.
We looked through the streets
like alleys, meant to confuse
thugs in the quarter for Jews.

That was quite enough
for us, walking up
the hill at noon.
No native would do that.

Later we lunched. We dealt
and discarded, laid down
and tallied again waiting for the train
we boarded at last and then

stepped down in Barcelona at the end
of day and that day's confusion.

ONE DAY NEAR AIX AND LATER

So many wrongs   so many slights
lasting afternoons   the linens
ruined   the languor
of one more midday excursion
while the locals napped   the fields
of artifacts   the occasional breeze

at the top of a valley
another Spartan defile.
This much is sure: we saw
broken columns   meadows
where legions fell in numbers
we can't know.

Pages of our guide blew
back and forth, and one
stood on edge in this photo
we kept: you at the fort
above a field of olives   the sun
lifting spikes of light on your arm.

Another day we carried
a wicker basket of bread
and tomatoes and wine from the clos
where S. was living
with his wife   her hooded eyes
as green as river stones.

We were all speaking
then   touring   looking
at various facts of art.
She left with the water-colorist—
that nonsense at Eaux Bonnes
in that hotel out of season

where she kept starting
another life. We had ours as before.
She waved good-bye as we made
for Brindisi   a rough crossing
but we ate   Turkish Delight
holding our own on the sticky deck.

THE SUMMER WE RULED VALENCIA

Let me say the flamenco last night was great
as far as I could see, and I am the King
of Spain for today, for months to come in fact:
we've let this swanky flat in the most regal,
most boisterous quarter of Valencia.
Our several balconies oversee a rock 'n' roll bar
two cafés and one dark shop, *Beat the Book,*
trafficking in Ginsberg and Kerouac.

Evenings we stroll to the flamenco club.
And last night! the floorboards were miked
so certain passes went off like gunshots.
PaPOW PaPOWPOW PaPOW danced
the principal. The woman reported POWee
KaPow Powee in smaller caliber.
But now
home again, in the near dawn, the hipsters
clatter and scatter from the bar. Balconies rattle.

All the while the assassin swallows peal
and swoop through the canyon of our street—
the *calle* of cowboys—sweeping up and down,
clearing the air—choreographies
of appetite. They snip past my seat in the loge.
In the old days when the river Turia muddled
close-by, the birds had more to pick from
and all summer the air was filled with stink.
But after one great flood the citizens stood up:

it's no small matter to move a river, but so
they did—south by southwest about four miles.
Olives in the valley never knew the difference,
but the swallows did.
                    They plunge and stoop,
Stukas of the winding air! These days *Turia*
labels a local beer and the river bed has become
a space for kids playing soccer and buskers
and dancers practicing. All of which we approve.

We are pleased to be rid largely of mosquitoes
and stench, to foster the arts and sport
in its place, but our time is up
at month's end. We need our rest.
We shall promise to abdicate . . .
as soon as the bar empties and its patrons
leave our street in peace
and the swallows have eaten their fill.

HEALTHY LIVING THREE

THE WALKING LOG

I. RESOLVE (3/27)

Exercise
today
takes me to the campus fields

where plugged to
lefty
radio I do my laps

and follow
cross talk
of nitrates   the cost of lives

and treasure.
No. Wait.
It's *night raids*. For a moment

I was lost
in odd
stresses and foreign rhythms.

Afghani
I guess.
We must review our options

the man says.
What else
do we ever do   I say.

Next topic:
SCOTUS
absurdest of acronyms

suggesting
scooters
or coitus or scrotum

in motion.
                                        Today's
gravitas concerns health care.

Obama's.
                                        Who knows
this? Cares? Sun   breeze   bikinis

the fields bright
                                        with flesh
balls on the pitch   balls in air.

I pause here
                                        because
I hear of death: Ms. Rich   gone.

Adrienne
                                        lost just
now. How is it I never knew

the first sound
                                        is "Awe"
not "A" simply? Not long. Gone.

Poet of
                                        anger
sex   politics rolled to one

and so railed

against
power and differentials

thereof. I
reverse
my route retracing fighting

fatigue. What
a drag
getting old getting the news

in hourly
segments
when you knew it all along.

No surprise
this sun,
azure skies clouds facing down

dealt across
the baize
mesa spreading toward Phoenix.

Good riddance
hands mucked.
I'll make the last cut run 'em

one more round
happy
to ante up see the flop.

ROTZY cadets
sprint
and rest   sprint and stretch   sprint and rest

and start over
wave
after orderly wave   cohorts

in motion. In
slow
motion   on the field south   a game

of softball ebbs
flows.
Lob. Thump. The ball hangs in the air

out of time   no
end.
The fresh young men make tracks as

I do my own.
Take
easy breaths. Every one

of us has next
things
in mind   our futures   rehearsing

for the perfect
test
perhaps tomorrow. This day's sun

breeze as before,
girls'
legs in vees spread on beach towels

flash of knee   thigh
all
the pretty ones lollygagging

on the infield
but
others   shy   soft   or simply lost

face away from
boys
running lines   the old guy circling.

III. AN INTERVIEW (7/10)

This interview though earbuds:
At first it's difficult for a white man

too aware of what went on
to "manage" (the word we choose to use here)

to manage a public land
(leaving aside earlier claims and such)

for the greatest good   greatest
number   so we have opportunities

galore   a new paradigm
setting down lighter footprints on the land

(here I think of softened hides
and piney woods)   for heavy bottom lines

cost benefits for us all.
Challenges of course   yes   those feral hogs

you mentioned once for instance.
They ruin the riparian zones   foul

the woods and   worse   spook tourists
our target customers   at the hot springs.

The wild hogs were imported
decades ago from Siberia   fine

sport for the hunting class   but
they have no natural predators here.

An alpine resort for them!
Ample food   fresh water   a few bears.

But we've managed challenges
before. It's our job. We offer trade-offs

each summer: some employment
for college kids (and locals if they want).

We teach them how to track and
trap and carry pigs elsewhere and rarely

in worst cases destroy them.
A win-win all around . . . except the pigs!

IV. CAMPUS PROGRESS (8/25)

No palaver today and still
great noise.
Industry. Progress.

Posted: Fugitive Dust Permit
No Hires
On This Site. Hard Hats!

They're finishing new dorms for fall,
stacking
cube on cube. Five floors.

Call it "Nuevo Pueblo"
hues of
stucco no one thought

before   puce and avocado
mauve mixed
with ordinary

colors of dirt. Called Casas del
Rio,
it's miles from water.

Who ever thought that adobe
box steps
could rise to such heights,

such flourish? Scaffolds crisscrossing,
façades,
more angles. Change comes

and goes all the same and we make
new things
from mud brick rebar

but ideas last too: In case
of siege,
pull up the ladders

save the children. They will escape
again
no matter no fear

of the dark. Inhale. Take this hill
at noon.
Down on the new courts

volleys echo in the instant
canyon.
Exhale. Two-thirds done.

V. ON THE MARCH AGAIN (9/17)

And so enter the students again:
class
fall rites football folderol.

Now in my ear falsetto Neil Young
croons
"Helpless" backed by rock 'n' roll

whose very soul Levon Helm (drummer
of
homely funk ostinatos

quick riffs of jump and change) has lately
left
us. Another departure.

I switch it off and step on the track's
grit
reverberating with the

waves of a marching band warming up
thritt
thritt-a-tit thritt-a-tit-tit.

Now the drummers the others still un-
pack-
ing instruments. Majorettes

unfurl pennants and begin to twirl
five
in a row grunting strutting

a palsy on the track as the brass
lines
assemble. My sneakers buzz.

Two cymbalists out of step offbeat
clang
whenever the spirit moves.

No time to ruminate now going
round
and back in clangor drummers,

dancers, and horns taking their places
down
the field making designs high-

stepping the ground broken by
                    green
          cadets. There are no yard lines

for guidance   no fans to recognize
                    shapes
          the band will form at halftime.

They're too close now to see for themselves.
                    Here
          comes a row of flutes   timpanists

picking nimbly through the divots   chunks
                    turf
          staying straight   counting each step

until they pivot away at the
                    edge
          of the track. We won't collide.

VI. IN HIS DAY (10/5)

Get on shank's mare   my dad said too often
          that's what I did   but

you can't be too sure. He liked saying things
          with a ring for what

the down home folks might say. A salesman through
          and through who wanted

to be one of the guys playing nine ball
          at Scotty's   smoking

Chesterfields   shooting the breeze. Take a hike.
    Hit the road. Beat feet.

Who never took a constitutional
    or anything else

fact is   for his health. Exercise was what
    you did lawn-mowing

or trimming the awful euonymus.
    Once he walked to work

when the Mercury got repossessed.
    But soon the contract

for bomb bay doors came through at Boeing
    giving him a raise

that let us keep the house in Riverside
    for another year.

My parents saved cigarette pack coupons
    shuffled them daily

paging through a catalog of rewards
    mail-order gadgets.

When I quit smoking and started running
    I ruined my knees

and that   I hear him say   just shows to go
    you   huh?   what you get:

that exercise will kill you. But not him.
    That was high balls.

VII. ONE END (12/31)

You see what comes of exercise: year's end   the plan,
            no surprise
                        scrapped.

Start again of course. You get x starts. If you knew
            how many
                        would

you stop counting   this log of interest mainly
            archival?
                        Save

the day tomorrow for resolve. Now take one step
            out the door
                        down

the alley. The next and so on. In these potholes
            the crazed ice
                        splits.

So much for winter. I grew up
            in Kansas
                        where

cold spells could kill you quickly. It's going to be
            something else
                        here.

            Reprise for
old Scotus the real. No joke.

Duns   that is
who gave to us the "thisness"

of a day
its particularity.

So notice
if you will a dusty sheen

on that crest.
His visions notwithstanding

the old coot
could not imagine this sky

this new world.
Oh! It's spring   lah   lah-ti-dah.

We made it
again! One more for us. Let

us muster
a genial gratitude.

IX. AN ANNIVERSARY (12/14)

It's brisk all right but not so cold it makes you want
to stand in the middle of your pants as Kansans put it

it's nothing to write home about. I zip my coat
and plug in the radio heading west into the wind

down the alley where now our self-absorbed road
runner struts north and south gravel edge to edge in rigid

belief he owns it all. He's looking for lizards
to snatch and brain. Our radio host reminds us a year

ago everything changed audio cut a small
voice: "it changed the wind riffling leaves the way they stirred" our hearts

broken for those who were all broken beyond our
hearts broken what we mean when words are not magic the way

we assume people know what we mean and stop talking.
Why I don't I don't know in consideration of all

that is possible. The road runner hops a wall
of puddled adobe bricks this bird that can fly but won't.

We can always talk. Our commentator suggests
we take violence as usual in ways we have come

to live with. At the corner of campus the "O"
has been lifted from the dorm sign: Casas del Ri_

Gibber. Children live here in concrete named for rivers:
Chama Jemez Pecos. Miles from here. Gibber. But children

live here I tell you Come one come all the children
miles from water unbroken children who live come one. All.

All
this exercise   counted or

not
lines and angles   circumstance

not-
withstanding   my summing up

goes
on. I am all for going

on
simply enough   day to day

not
in the manner of constant

news
misconstrued   a daily nod

to
how things are (numbing, is it

not?)
but with noticing with some

care
parsing this and that and that's

all
I am asking for right now.

THE ARTS FOUR

YOU WENT TO THE PRADO

Say something pleasant in the tavern
in the restaurant   in the café   whatever
it is you say   whatever you call this place
across the broad *calle* to the Prado.

A woman asked a question
you could not answer.
                    Say instead
you saw the Goyas today
as well as works by Velasquez
severe buffoons   his "people of pleasure"
in corsets and snoods and fine threads
and later in nearby rooms
plenty of nipples   fresh symmetries
for the next century.
                    You never know
about women you see in the *museo*
in the intimate air of close rooms
shared observations. You never know
who they are who speak so quietly
you can't discern the language
arm in arm   picture to picture
whispering. There were three women
in front of the Graces of Rubens
with dimpling thighs.
                    One might have been
that woman in the café   in the restaurant.
She was Italian   left-handed   managing
her paella with a backward flourish.
                              She asked
in English, "Is this rabbit or squirrel?"
As if you knew! She fought the small claws
tooth and nail   sucking each one dry.

In the last room you saw
Goya again a pair of old men
eating supper except the one
on the right can't be alive his hand
on the spoon so rigorous.
Stubborn appetite!
On the facing wall his dog sinks
in a rusty muck looking for help from above
which is a shapeless yellow space.

You certainly did not meet in that room.
Think what you might have seen
together—ruff and bustle and fine flush
ruined. Instead you walked outside alone
past the statue of Goya the great one
and across the street to this place.

The woman cleaned her plate scraping
the *pegado* with her knife's edge.

She said
I saw you in the room of pillage.
And I saw you
in the room of despair you answered
in the room of appetite where
I saw the bony end of men and a dog looking
to heaven which I would say is a yellow bog.

LOSING SLEEP IN THE LITTLE BALKANS

I.

Not a word all night, but now at dawn
the elms stand around, airing it out,
bristling, sighs of rumor, news—
gossip or catastrophe. Who knows
this early in the day? I take a guess,
penciling in some thrilled flesh,
but then take it out. Ditto the bruise-
colored clouds I can actually see
as wide as a field of alfalfa
without lightning, which I've seen
a thousand times. I listen for thunder.
Nothing rings true along those lines,
but the starlings are squawking
about territory. And the jay, of course.

II.

The stories women tell, intricate
as they are and made of more words
than pictures, will never help me sleep.
At night, listening, I know quiet things
are going on in the alley, scampering
and nudging. I know the ruinous canopies
huddle and grow in leaf and loam.
I go out there afternoons to read
the trails, kicking at toadstools,
leaving stubs of stalk thick as thumbs.
I am weak on cause and effect.
I know more will grow. And I know
it's lust or a cat that drives the squirrels
clacking from oak to mimosa and back.

III.

The honeysuckle thickens,
taking my breath in season.
I should stay in. Yesterday in the alley
I was casting about for a story
in the heavy air, in a fan dance
of mimosas that were hung with cicadas
ugly and dense as the plugs
we use, fishing for bass in pools
left behind by strip mining. The land
is only fit for milo. Nothing else.
I have said plenty of times
you should never eat those fish.
I'm saying now: I am the last to get
the news no matter how long I'm awake.

IV.

I'm listening to the cicadas
dragging their woeful song
from oak to mimosa and back.
It's a love story from three-note
lotharios with nothing to lose.
Numbskulls. But you can't
blame them for such
a lousy adolescence.
No choice. No choice.
No choice. Your own life begins
to take on another life
with a new anthem, a tune
too thin to sing out loud.
Be quiet. Lie still. Listen.

V.

That's probably enough prophecy
and what it comes to. I go running,
jog-trotting down Jefferson after a rain.
Seeing a lump in the gutter, I leap
to the parking, alarmed, imagining
a bloated squirrel, smelling disease.
But no. Only rotting leaves. These days
the light leaves early. We are saving time.
But whose? The time of my other life—
work, the money of other people. Fall
is ugly everywhere. God's ugliest things,
the starlings, begin to gather at the top
of a hollow elm, hammering the underside
of sky, dull as tin. Bang. Bang. Get on home.

VI.

Review the day, the office voodoo.
Somebody's dollars given over,
reinvested. A shower, a shampoo,
a double martini. Whatever you do,
don't worry about the kids everyone
else does. Who doubts the essential health
of children doubts too the appointed place
of god, the equator, and the Eiffel Tower.
This is not one of my daffier thoughts.
But some days can be explained in cracked
syntax, fortunes from the House of Hunan.
"Whatever you think can't happen can't."
But consider a period. ". . . can't happen.
Can't." That's the rumor anyway.

READING PALMS: INTRODUCTION

You can study this hand
all you want. For that matter, the other.

I have no objection but time
wasted both ways, but if

you find a pattern of accident,
oxymoronic as that may be,

a series of mistakes you believe
add up, keep it to yourself.

This destiny riff—star, stone,
a crease of oil—doesn't cut it.

All I see is one bloody idea
after another: a fish hook,

a fistfight or two, a trigger
pulled or released. Nothing ordained.

Whatever plots you concoct
don't connect the scars

I made all by myself. I remain
committed to the daily give-and-take.

As for fancier signs—
your bracelets and tassels—

I swapped my gee-gaws
and bangles a long time ago.

Given your hustle, you can invent,
no doubt, a hero of certain ambiguity,

a time and place and honest-
to-goodness detail. It won't be mine.

I'll take the thickened skin for now,
save the immutable for tomorrow.

BOOKISH NOIR

What mystery fans know—no coincidence
can be mere and nothing left to chance—
makes for a good read bound to make sense.

We all know there's every reason to finish
another one and the next: we accomplish
each tedious review of facts because we wish

old plots of our own were so clear, so neatly
committed. In that case we could explain easily
over cocktails how we came to be *here* exactly

not there, friends and enemies alike listening,
laughing when we say the body's still missing.
Not even the perp can recall her issue

her motive. Let's face it: we don't know why—
this place, that baby face, which campus? It went by
without chapter, verse, or obvious anomaly.

That's why we read the good read and go to sleep
knowing something is over. Why we wake up
ready for another caper, a last scrap.

READING PALMS: SLEIGHT OF HAND

In this palm the sign
of a small pain almost forgotten:
a ragged tear x-ing the spot
where I fell on a log
crossing a luminous creek
of rainbows.
                    Sponged and sewed
the wound gave back
days later a chunk of bark,
old-growth pine thick
as a matchstick and the color
of smoke. It split the skin;
another stitch.

Now here's another flaw
below my ring finger,
a tiny twist of skin. At age six
I shot myself by mistake,
cocking a pistol used for races.
Point-blank the paper wad
tore the flesh and mixed it
with black powder and blood,
foaming a furious color
I'd never seen.
                    I ran home
sure that some part was lost.
But no. More stitches
and Mercurochrome made
a garish mauve that turned green
the next day, but it dried tannish
and puckered after that: a dust
devil on the Plain of Mars.

But that first color—
before any palmist saw
destinies in a trace—never
left me. I saw it again
decades later—explosions
roiling on canvas,
a battle at sea by Turner—
smoke and fire fixed
to a wall, a sky pitted
like flesh forever.

ONE OF DAUMIER'S DON QUIXOTES

This time they've just come through
the pass. The plain spreads out below.
I believe it is evening—that suffusion
of orange on the horizon.

For now, they have arrived,
but Sancho may not know this,
slumping, snoozing as he is,
a shapely smudge on his mule.

For now he has not disappeared.
He has his place and his shadow
etched on the outcrop. Tonight
he will not dream about tomorrow

nor recall this plain below,
as empty as yesterday's, as full
of second chances as the one the day before.
Sancho has no plans.

The plain spreads out below,
empty except for the trees,
the definite trees I believe are olives,
given the landscape and what I know.

There will be several versions more
before Sancho disappears,
his body not even a shrug.
The don will be alone, severe

and angular and ascetic
in stricken lines, a lance as thin
and limber as a sapling.
without buds. And useless.

There is no gesture as empty
as the plain spread out below,
marked by definite trees.
How do I dare say this?

The don has no need of Sancho
now, has no hunger pangs
which Sancho was good for.
Perhaps olives to eat tomorrow.

LABOR DAY AT THE PARK

I would never guess that so many
come here
on a day off to watch butterflies sail and glide

alight. O   look   Mom   Dad   what is that
blue one?
Monarchs everywhere and all manner of crawling things

that may or may not grow wings   become
something
else. How does that work? So many have come here today

to a rickety pavilion   just
a frame
in fact   fitted with mosquito netting   a screen door

slapping   and slapping. A volunteer
lady
fidgets every time a kid lets go of it   sits

close inside to pull it shut. "Just this
morning
we unloaded crates of fresh butterflies from Brazil,"

she smiles   smiles. "We hope they like it here."
Of course.
A far cry from work! A day with kids   wife   the whole place

breathing easily. A susurrus.
Squabbles
at the family cookout avoided. So later

a steak as rare as you want   your sister
not there.
It's not that you don't love her or the kids. Not at all.

There are no cucaracha s today.
These are
niña de la Tierre   not really anything like them.

Look closely. Just ugly's all,
but not
something to shy from. Brought up by the heavy rainfall

they don't like you any more than you
like them.
Live and let live   kids. We'll never know much if we don't

look twice. What if all these butterflies
took a
powder at once, changed matters in our hemisphere?

I think I can feel the beat of wings
if I
stand still. I like the idea of quiet chaos

better than the noise of making
things work.
It's true   approximately anything may happen

next. Still we can't carry on like that
for long.
We need some elements settled. Otherwise nothing

makes sense. More kids stand in the doorway.
Hurry
Grampa   won't you   come on. Shut the door please   quickly please

don’t let them all go oh no   snatching
                                        the screen
shut. See that yellow one   Grampa? When the door slaps shut

the butterflies scatter just as if
                                        old Vlad
great white Russian drunk on exhibits   were coming behind

waving his net   eyeballing beauty
                                        or just
as when I surprised some drinking the juice of salmon

washed up on a stream in autumn in Oregon
                                        or just
as I watched them all turn from leaves to clouds on Paros

fifty years ago. Each occasion
                                        surely
caused something else and so on   after we were gone.

THE BROTHERS TIME HAVE MADE A MOVIE

The Brothers Time have made a movie
about what happens. Almost.
Not quite. What they have made: notes
and more notes: scenes, locations,
dialogue. High- and melodrama, slapstick,
rom-com, Hitchcock to Chaplin.
                                        They flirted
with comic book heroes and cartoons,
but they craved something fleshier,
something with flaws. Now and then, noticing
the bingeing craze on TV, they considered
settling for a series, endless renewals.
But no: old school in the end, they knew
that classic problems involve classic solutions,
beginning and end, and even perhaps apocalypse.
And so they make more notes, filing them in archival
boxes on custom shelves along the basement wall
opposite the washer and dryer.
                                        How long has this
been going on?
                    "It's progress," says the young one,
on their lunch break, but Senior doesn't see it
anymore. Where does it all *go*? he says.
What happens next and so on, so it's inevitable
and fresh at once? Not to mention done with?
Junior, slicing his Fugi, doesn't know yet.
In media res. The work's enough for now.

Senior pushes for agreement: Can you agree,
whatever the end, it must be slam-bang? No sequels?

For Senior, it's worn thin, this clocking in,
clocking out, and weekends off. His work
has turned sloppy. Last Tuesday he lost
an entire decade overnight, misfiled
in a system become too intricate
with references, indices, color coding.

So these days at day's end he leaves
the files on top of the washer for Junior
to review and put back. They can't afford
the time lost should he forget again.
Senior couldn't care less. He thinks
everything's connected one way
or another, if not always in time exactly.
He sees today for instance that "refile"
and "rifle" are largely the same. And "riffle."
Is that coincidence?
                                        About 5 he takes a double martini
and his dog, who happens to be a spoiled retriever (!),
to the front patio. They pay no mind
to the keyboard of industry clacking away inside.
Out here stories drift through the air
the dog sniffs.
                          Sometimes passersby wave
and call out and other animals come close.
The dog, too, is old, and lumpy with warts.
His beautiful black flews have faded.
So what? Senior says out loud,
The older he gets, the older he gets.

Etcetera. Ephemera. Lacunae.
Empty parens—each blank space an emphasis.
Memory need not serve. He can't find the place
for certain words he knows mean something.

Now an interruption: an oath from inside.
The unoiled cabinet door slams shut.
Another moment unaccounted for . . .
He has done this all before! Whatever
happened to the daily test of gratitude?
Just then, just now he notices
the desert willow waving good-bye in the breeze
above, and below the rabbit bush nodding
a counter rhythm, full of grace, full of sway.

READING PALMS: INCANTATION

The line   below the fold
The line   runs below the fold
The line for the head runs below the fold

        for the heart   above   life
        for the heart and above the line of life
of that for the heart and above the line of life

          fades   the older
before it fades   because the older
before it fades south. Because the older

you get the more   broken
you get   more interruptions   broken
you get the more interruptions the one broken

                                           for instance
line or another   scars for instance
line or another means little. Scars for instance

         a callus   changes   the story
or even a callus   changes   the story
or even a callus may spell changes in the story

               set in   soft flesh
          not set in stone   but soft flesh
which is not set in stone after all, but soft flesh

and so the   unfolding
and so the   plot unfolding becomes
and so the analysis of plot unfolding becomes

          less   foretold
more or less postmodern   foretold
more or less postmodern and not foretold

Take this line   cut
Take this line for my heart cut lately
Take this line for my heart cut lately twice

and repair   sutures bristling
and repair   sutures bristling in my palm
and repaired, blue sutures bristling in my palm

like antennae   below
like antennae on   wounds below
like antennae on the insect of wounds below the

                      middle finger and   pinky
long and short   middle finger and   pinky
long and short of it, middle finger and the pinky

triggers   released
triggers locked   now released
triggers locked mornings but now released

so I can   grip
so I can make a fist   a grip
so I can make a fist again, get a grip

             shake   in greeting
         and shake a hand in greeting
on a cup and shake a hand in greeting.

ACKNOWLEDGMENTS

These poems, sometimes in other versions, appeared in the following journals:

200 New Mexico Poems: "An Osprey on the Stream"
Alibi: A Calendar" (last two sections)
ABQ InPrint: "Reading Palms: Sleight of Hand,"
and "Reading Palms: Incantation"
bosque: "You Went to the Prado"
Coal City Review: "What She Said"
Hampden-Sydney Poetry Review: "Road Trip Home"
and "You Can See on This Postcard"
Mikrokosmos: "Concerning Certain Deaths in Rural America"
Nimrod: "Garbage"
Shenandoah: "Poverty Point" and "Rotogravure from Sounion"
Weaving the Territory: "Owl Made in China"

A NOTE ON "THE WALKING LOG" POEMS

The poems in The Walking Log represent journal entries for particular days as indicated in the parenthesis after each title. Originally I meant for the "log" to be a form of exercise or discipline, and I decided to use a syllabic scheme that would replicate the date of the entry. For example, the first poem, "Resolve," is dated (3/27). The syllabic lines then are three syllables, two syllables, and seven syllables for a three-line stanza. That stanza form, then, is repeated through the poem. I found that this arbitrary formal imposition created a kind of freedom by forcing me to look at new constructions and words.

CPSIA information can be obtained
at www.ICGtesting.com
Printed in the USA
LVHW030338310122
709391LV00003B/11